The Most Common Business Expressions

EXPRESSION: *24/7*

MEANING: 24 hours a day, 7 days a week.

EXAMPLE: My boss must think I'm a robot. I could work 24/7 and it still wouldn't be enough for him!

EXPRESSION:

MEANING:

EXAMPLES:

EXPRESSION: a tough break

MEANING: an unfortunate event or bad luck

EXAMPLE: It was a tough break for the marketing department when their salaries got cut.

EXPRESSION:

MEANING:

EXAMPLES:

EXPRESSION: ahead of the curve

MEANING: to be more advanced or better prepared than the competition

EXAMPLE: Industry leaders are always ahead of the curve when it comes to innovation.

EXPRESSION:

MEANING:

EXAMPLES:

EXPRESSION: ahead of the pack

MEANING: in the lead or ahead of your group or competitors

EXAMPLE: Our company has one rule for leadership: stay ahead of the pack.

EXPRESSION:

MEANING:

EXAMPLES:

EXPRESSION: ASAP

MEANING: as soon as possible

EXAMPLE: Get that proposal to me ASAP.

EXPRESSION:

MEANING:

EXAMPLES:

EXPRESSION: at stake

MEANING: at risk of losing

EXAMPLE: Our entire investment is at stake with the production delays.

EXPRESSION:

MEANING:

EXAMPLES:

EXPRESSION: back to square one

MEANING: starting over from the beginning

EXAMPLE: Our investor rejected our marketing plan, so we're back to square one.

EXPRESSION:

MEANING:

EXAMPLES:

EXPRESSION: back to the drawing board

MEANING: to return to the planning stage

EXAMPLE: The Wright Brothers had to go back to the drawing board again and again until they designed a plane that could actually fly.

EXPRESSION:

MEANING:

EXAMPLES:

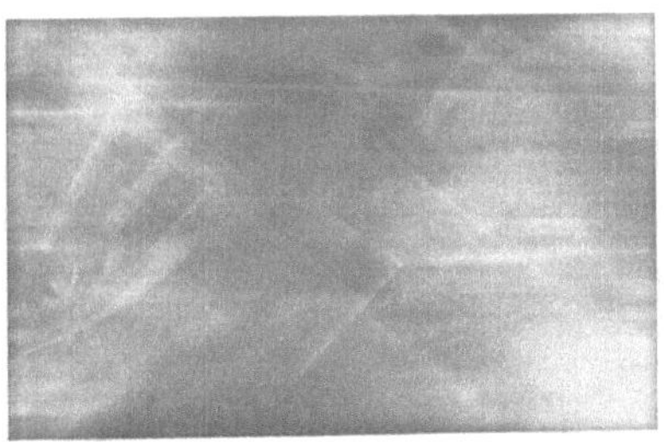

EXPRESSION: backroom deal

MEANING: an agreement or decision made without the public knowing about it

EXAMPLE: Much of what gets done in politics is the result of backroom deals.

EXPRESSION:

MEANING:

EXAMPLES:

EXPRESSION: ballpark number/figure

MEANING: a very rough estimate

EXAMPLE: Give me a ballpark number for how much money this project will cost us.

EXPRESSION:

MEANING:

EXAMPLES:

EXPRESSION: behind someone's back

MEANING: to sneakily do something without someone's knowledge

EXAMPLE: She acts like my friend, but goes behind my back and criticizes me to our boss and coworkers.

EXPRESSION:

MEANING:

EXAMPLES:

EXPRESSION: behind the scenes

MEANING: what happens outside of public view or in secret

EXAMPLE: It takes a lot of work behind the scenes to make a presentation a success.

EXPRESSION:

MEANING:

EXAMPLES:

EXPRESSION: big picture

MEANING: an overall or panoramic view of something

EXAMPLE: A good stock forecaster looks at the big picture, not just the P&L statements.

EXPRESSION:

MEANING:

EXAMPLES:

EXPRESSION: blue collar worker

MEANING: someone who works with their hands (manufacturing, construction, maintenance, etc.)

EXAMPLE: He's a blue collar worker that works hard, long hours without complaint.

EXPRESSION:

MEANING:

EXAMPLES:

EXPRESSION: white collar worker

MEANING: someone who works in an office (bank, HR, management, sales, etc.)

EXAMPLE: The project manager is a white collar worker but isn't afraid to get his hands dirty when a job needs done.

EXPRESSION:

MEANING:

EXAMPLES:

EXPRESSION: by the book

MEANING: to strictly follow the rules, company policy, or the law

EXAMPLE: We are regularly audited by tax authorities so it's important we do everything by the book to prevent problems.

EXPRESSION:

MEANING:

EXAMPLES:

EXPRESSION: call it a day

MEANING: to stop work for the day

EXAMPLE: We've been working nonstop. Let's call it a day and go get drinks.

EXPRESSION:

MEANING:

EXAMPLES:

EXPRESSION: catch someone off guard

MEANING: to surprise someone with something they are not expecting

EXAMPLE: I'm going to arrive an hour early to catch them off guard.

EXPRESSION:

MEANING:

EXAMPLES:

EXPRESSION: cave/cave in

MEANING: to agree to something or give in to a request that was previously denied

EXAMPLE: How can I get my boss to cave and give me a bigger raise?

EXPRESSION:

MEANING:

EXAMPLES:

EXPRESSION: change of pace

MEANING: a change in the normal routine or schedule

EXAMPLE: We need a change of pace to get our employees motivated again.

EXPRESSION:

MEANING:

EXAMPLES:

EXPRESSION: came up short

MEANING: to try to achieve something but partially fail

EXAMPLE: We came up short on the annual sales goals so the company has put a freeze on all new hires and travel.

EXPRESSION:

MEANING:

EXAMPLES:

EXPRESSION: corner the market

MEANING: to dominate a particular market

EXAMPLE: Apple cornered the market on smart phones when they developed the iPhone.

EXPRESSION:

MEANING:

EXAMPLES:

EXPRESSION: cut corners

MEANING: to take shortcuts and find an easier way to finish something, usually unethically

EXAMPLE: My coworker is lazy and always tries to cut corners.

EXPRESSION:

MEANING:

EXAMPLES:

EXPRESSION: cut one's losses

MEANING: to stop unproductive activities that won't ever generate results

EXAMPLE: I'm going to cut my losses and sell all my stock in that company before I lose everything.

EXPRESSION:

MEANING:

EXAMPLES:

EXPRESSION: cut-throat

MEANING: a situation that is very intense, aggressive, merciless, and uncompassionate

EXAMPLE: Interviewing and getting hired on Wall Street can be very cut-throat.

EXPRESSION:

MEANING:

EXAMPLES:

EXPRESSION: diamond in the rough

MEANING: something or someone that has a lot of potential but first requires a lot of work

EXAMPLE: Ann is a diamond in the rough. She is hard working, intelligent, and creative and will be really successful once she improves her communication skills.

EXPRESSION:

MEANING:

EXAMPLES:

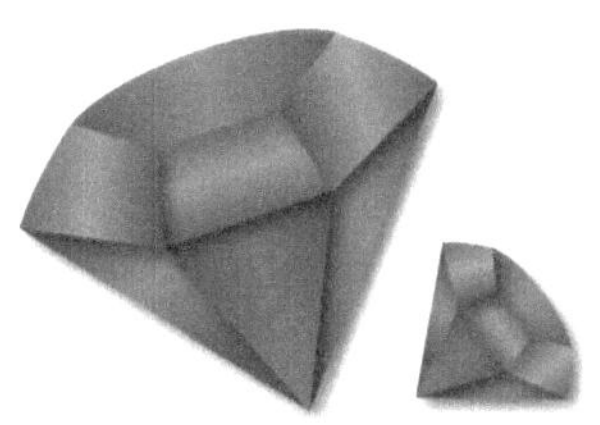

EXPRESSION: easy come, easy go

MEANING: something that comes easily is often lost easily

EXAMPLE: His approach to money was easy come, easy go, which is why he ended up in debt.

EXPRESSION:

MEANING:

EXAMPLES:

EXPRESSION: fifty-fifty

MEANING: divided equally, 50% for one party, 50% for the other

EXAMPLE: My housemate and I split the expenses fifty-fifty.

EXPRESSION:

MEANING:

EXAMPLES:

EXPRESSION: from the ground up

MEANING: starting with nothing or very little to work with

EXAMPLE: Ray Kroc didn't invent McDonald's hamburgers, but he built the company from the ground up.

EXPRESSION:

MEANING:

EXAMPLES:

EXPRESSION: game plan

MEANING: a strategy or plan of action

EXAMPLE: We're developing a game plan for next year's pharmaceutical marketing and sales campaign.

EXPRESSION:

MEANING:

EXAMPLES:

EXPRESSION: get back in/into the swing of things

MEANING: to get used to doing something again after having a break from that activity

EXAMPLE: After weeks on holiday, it's hard to get back in the swing of things at the office.

EXPRESSION:

MEANING:

EXAMPLES:

EXPRESSION: get down to business

MEANING: to stop making small talk or wasting time and start talking or getting serious about important business matters

EXAMPLE: I don't have much time so let's get down to business.

EXPRESSION:

MEANING:

EXAMPLES:

EXPRESSION: get something off the ground

MEANING: to get something started, like a project or business

EXAMPLE: I am glad the planning process is over and am ready to get the project off the ground.

EXPRESSION:

MEANING:

EXAMPLES:

EXPRESSION: get the ball rolling

MEANING: to start something or build momentum, like a project or campaign

EXAMPLE: I need to get a job so I can get the ball rolling on my career.

EXPRESSION:

MEANING:

EXAMPLES:

EXPRESSION: get/be/stay on their good side

MEANING: when someone likes or respects you

EXAMPLE: I need to stay on their good side so they will renew their contract.

EXPRESSION:

MEANING:

EXAMPLES:

EXPRESSION: get/have one's foot in the door

MEANING: to take a low-level position in hopes of eventually getting a promotion

EXAMPLE: Many students take internship positions before graduation to get their foot in the door with large companies.

EXPRESSION:

MEANING:

EXAMPLES:

EXPRESSION: give someone a pat on the back

MEANING: to give praise or approval:

EXAMPLE: Our boss gave us a pat on the back for the profitable marketing results.

EXPRESSION:

MEANING:

EXAMPLES:

EXPRESSION: a thumbs down

MEANING: to disapprove

EXAMPLE: The stupid marketing team gave my PowerPoint presentation a thumbs down!

EXPRESSION:

MEANING:

EXAMPLES:

EXPRESSION: a thumbs up

MEANING: to approve

EXAMPLE: The client gave us a thumbs up so we start tomorrow.

EXPRESSION:

MEANING:

EXAMPLES:

EXPRESSION: go for broke

MEANING: to take a risk that may result in bankruptcy or losing everything on a business or venture

EXAMPLE: We're all in at this point so I say let's take our chances and go for broke.

EXPRESSION:

MEANING:

EXAMPLES:

EXPRESSION: go down the drain

MEANING: to waste or lose resources

EXAMPLE: All my hard work went down the drain when my new boss canceled my project.

EXPRESSION:

MEANING:

EXAMPLES:

EXPRESSION: go the extra mile

MEANING: to do more than what people expect

EXAMPLE: I often go the extra mile for my clients by calling them to make sure they are pleased with the product.

EXPRESSION:

MEANING:

EXAMPLES:

EXPRESSION: go through the roof

MEANING: to rapidly increase -or- is very upset

EXAMPLE: Our profits went through the roof last quarter -or- My wife went through the roof when she saw how much I spent on front row tickets.

EXPRESSION:

MEANING:

EXAMPLES:

EXPRESSION: gray area

MEANING: something that is not clearly defined or easily categorized

EXAMPLE: I asked our accountant if it's legal and she said it's a gray area.

EXPRESSION:

MEANING:

EXAMPLES:

EXPRESSION: ground-breaking

MEANING: not just new and innovative, but life changing or industry changing

EXAMPLE: Harvard researcher David Sinclair made ground-breaking discoveries on increasing life expectancy.

EXPRESSION:

MEANING:

EXAMPLES:

EXPRESSION: hands are tied

MEANING: no control over a situation

EXAMPLE: I signed a non-compete agreement so my hands are tied. I can't take that great job with their competitor.

EXPRESSION:

MEANING:

EXAMPLES:

EXPRESSION: have someone's work cut out

MEANING: having a particularly difficult assignment or lot

EXAMPLE: She has very high standards, so you'll have your work cut out if you want to impress her at the board meeting tomorrow.

EXPRESSION:

MEANING:

EXAMPLES:

EXPRESSION: hit the nail on the head

MEANING: to do or say something 100% correctly or accurately

EXAMPLE: I agree with George 100%. He really hit the nail on the head.

EXPRESSION:

MEANING:

EXAMPLES:

EXPRESSION: in a nutshell

MEANING: in summary or in a few words

EXAMPLE: In a nutshell, this book is about business expressions.

EXPRESSION:

MEANING:

EXAMPLES:

EXPRESSION: in full swing

MEANING: working at full capacity or full speed

EXAMPLE: The water bottling factory will be in full swing by the end of this month.

EXPRESSION:

MEANING:

EXAMPLES:

EXPRESSION: in the black

MEANING: making a profit or earning more than expenses

EXAMPLE: It's going to be years before this startup company sells enough products to be in the black.

EXPRESSION:

MEANING:

EXAMPLES:

EXPRESSION: in the driver's seat

MEANING: in control

EXAMPLE: I'm used to being in the driver's seat but now I need to adapt to having a manager.

EXPRESSION:

MEANING:

EXAMPLES:

EXPRESSION: in the red

MEANING: in debt or operating at a loss

EXAMPLE: I'm in the red because I spend more than my paycheck on shopping and eating out.

EXPRESSION:

MEANING:

EXAMPLES:

EXPRESSION: keep one's eye on the ball

MEANING: to give full attention and focus

EXAMPLE: The politicians have to keep their eye on the ball about the new tax plan.

EXPRESSION:

MEANING:

EXAMPLES:

EXPRESSION: last straw

MEANING: to push over the edge

EXAMPLE: Jim showing up late for the big presentation was the last straw. I'm firing him tomorrow.

EXPRESSION:

MEANING:

EXAMPLES:

EXPRESSION: learn the ropes

MEANING: to learn the basics

EXAMPLE: I had to learn the ropes as an intern before I could get my first real job.

EXPRESSION:

MEANING:

EXAMPLES:

EXPRESSION: long shot

MEANING: something that is unlikely or improbable to occur

EXAMPLE: Winning the lottery is a long shot, but millions of people still buy lottery tickets.

EXPRESSION:

MEANING:

EXAMPLES:

EXPRESSION: loophole

MEANING: lack of legal clarity, allowing people or corporations to take often unintended advantage of laws and rules

EXAMPLE: He hardly pays taxes because he hires smart accountants to help him find loopholes in tax laws.

EXPRESSION:

MEANING:

EXAMPLES:

EXPRESSION: lose ground (opposite: gain ground)

MEANING: to lose your standing, advantage, market share, or position

EXAMPLE: The banking industry is gradually losing ground to Financial Technologies.

EXPRESSION:

MEANING:

EXAMPLES:

EXPRESSION: lose-lose / no-win situation

MEANING: every option or possible course of action will have a negative outcome

EXAMPLE: People will be angry if they cut government programs and they'll be angry if they raise taxes, but it has to be one or the other. It's a lose-lose situation.

EXPRESSION:

MEANING:

EXAMPLES:

EXPRESSION: a nine-to-five

MEANING: a job based on the standard work day that starts at 9 a.m. and ends at 5 p.m.

EXAMPLE: I chose to be a waiter because I couldn't handle the monotony of a nine-to-five.

EXPRESSION:

MEANING:

EXAMPLES:

EXPRESSION: no brainer

MEANING: a decision or action that doesn't require much thought or has an obvious solution

EXAMPLE: His qualifications are so good, hiring him is a no brainer.

EXPRESSION:

MEANING:

EXAMPLES:

EXPRESSION: no strings attached

MEANING: no expectation of anything in return for a gift or gesture

EXAMPLE: My coworker bought me a coffee, no strings attached. I thought she was going to ask for help on a project but she didn't ask for anything in return.

EXPRESSION:

MEANING:

EXAMPLES:

EXPRESSION: no time to lose

MEANING: heavy pressure to finish by a deadline

EXAMPLE: There's no time to lose, we have to get this done today.

EXPRESSION:

MEANING:

EXAMPLES:

EXPRESSION: not going to fly

MEANING: not going to be accepted or is ineffective

EXAMPLE: With increased costs and smaller profits, it's not going to fly with the boss.

EXPRESSION:

MEANING:

EXAMPLES:

EXPRESSION: off the top of one's head

MEANING: responding without thinking too much or researching the subject

EXAMPLE: I have no idea what the population of the UK is but off the top of my head, I'd say about 55 million.

EXPRESSION:

MEANING:

EXAMPLES:

EXPRESSION: on a roll

MEANING: multiple successes in a row

EXAMPLE: I saw you just had your 5th big sale this month. You're on a roll!

EXPRESSION:

MEANING:

EXAMPLES:

EXPRESSION: on the ball

MEANING: to be alert, aware, or on top of things

EXAMPLE: You're really on the ball with planning this event. It's sure to run smoothly because of you.

EXPRESSION:

MEANING:

EXAMPLES:

EXPRESSION: on the same page

MEANING: in agreement or a shared understanding about a particular topic

EXAMPLE: The liberals and conservatives are definitely not on the same page about the tax plan.

EXPRESSION:

MEANING:

EXAMPLES:

EXPRESSION: on top of something

MEANING: in control of a situation, or aware of the latest news and developments

EXAMPLE: To be the best doctor I can be, I read a lot to stay on top of the latest medical research.

EXPRESSION:

MEANING:

EXAMPLES:

EXPRESSION: on your toes

MEANING: to be alert and observant

EXAMPLE: I have to stay on my toes or my sneaky coworker might take my job!

EXPRESSION:

MEANING:

EXAMPLES:

EXPRESSION: out in the open

MEANING: is public knowledge and transparent

EXAMPLE: Usually, it's best to be out in the open to avoid integrity and trust issues in the future.

EXPRESSION:

MEANING:

EXAMPLES:

EXPRESSION: out of the loop (opposite: in the loop)

MEANING: to not know something that a select group of people know

EXAMPLE: I felt like I was out of the loop after being away for three weeks.

EXPRESSION:

MEANING:

EXAMPLES:

EXPRESSION: pink slip

MEANING: a document that terminates employment

EXAMPLE: I wish I could give my boss a pink slip and take his job.

EXPRESSION:

MEANING:

EXAMPLES:

EXPRESSION: play hardball

MEANING: to be competitive, aggressive, and merciless, doing anything to win

EXAMPLE: When you get in the big leagues of business, people play hardball.

EXPRESSION:

MEANING:

EXAMPLES:

EXPRESSION: put all one's eggs in one basket

MEANING: to put all resources and energy into one venture or investment

EXAMPLE: Warren Buffet advises to never put all your eggs in one basket and to instead diversify your stocks portfolio.

EXPRESSION:

MEANING:

EXAMPLES:

EXPRESSION: put the cart before the horse

MEANING: to get ahead of yourself, getting priorities out of order

EXAMPLE: You're putting the cart before the horse if you start a business without a solid business plan.

EXPRESSION:

MEANING:

EXAMPLES:

EXPRESSION: raise the bar

MEANING: to increase standards and expectations

EXAMPLE: Our boss is raising the bar this year when it comes to sales. We have to increase sales by 3% in Spain this year.

EXPRESSION:

MEANING:

EXAMPLES:

EXPRESSION: read between the lines

MEANING: to understand something that is implied, not communicated directly

EXAMPLE: If you read between the lines of our boss's "pep talk", we're going to be fired if we don't make our sales.

EXPRESSION:

MEANING:

EXAMPLES:

EXPRESSION: red tape

MEANING: excessive rules, procedures, regulations, and paperwork usually used to deter, distract, or delay people or businesses

EXAMPLE: Some countries have so much red tape that they scare away foreign investors.

EXPRESSION:

MEANING:

EXAMPLES:

EXPRESSION: rock the boat

MEANING: cause problems and disrupt the peaceful and normal flow of things

EXAMPLE: I don't want to rock the boat but who approved this project in the first place? We're going to lose a ton of money on it.

EXPRESSION:

MEANING:

EXAMPLES:

EXPRESSION: round-the-clock

MEANING: 24 hours a day, 7 days a week

EXAMPLE: BSH in Zaragoza manufactures round-the-clock during peak seasons.

EXPRESSION:

MEANING:

EXAMPLES:

EXPRESSION: run/go around in circles

MEANING: to do the same thing over and over without any results

EXAMPLE: We are running around in circles arguing about how to reduce the budget for next quarter.

EXPRESSION:

MEANING:

EXAMPLES:

EXPRESSION: safe bet

MEANING: a certainty, or very high probability

EXAMPLE: It's a safe bet that people will live longer as medicine advances.

EXPRESSION:

MEANING:

EXAMPLES:

EXPRESSION: same boat

MEANING: in the same situation

EXAMPLE: We're all in the same boat, worrying about losing our jobs.

EXPRESSION:

MEANING:

EXAMPLES:

EXPRESSION: second nature

MEANING: when you have done something so many times or for so long it doesn't require much thought or effort to do

EXAMPLE: With 20 years of experience, teaching kindergarten is second nature to her.

EXPRESSION:

MEANING:

EXAMPLES:

EXPRESSION: see eye to eye

MEANING: to agree with someone's opinion or method

EXAMPLE: I don't see eye to eye with my boss when it comes to managing the sales floor.

EXPRESSION:

MEANING:

EXAMPLES:

EXPRESSION: see something through

MEANING: to complete or finish

EXAMPLE: I really want to see this through before starting another project.

EXPRESSION:

MEANING:

EXAMPLES:

EXPRESSION: sever ties

MEANING: to cut contact with someone

EXAMPLE: After the company treated us that way, it's time to sever ties and move on.

EXPRESSION:

MEANING:

EXAMPLES:

EXPRESSION: shoot something down

MEANING: to reject a proposal or idea

EXAMPLE: You should listen carefully before you shoot down someone's ideas, especially during a brainstorming session.

EXPRESSION:

MEANING:

EXAMPLES:

EXPRESSION: sky's the limit

MEANING: no limit to what you can achieve

EXAMPLE: With the internet, the sky's the limit as to what information you can find.

EXPRESSION:

MEANING:

EXAMPLES:

EXPRESSION: small talk

MEANING: conversation about unimportant topics, such as the weather, especially to break the ice when meeting someone

EXAMPLE: A few minutes of small talk can help you connect with others before moving on to business matters.

EXPRESSION:

MEANING:

EXAMPLES:

EXPRESSION: smooth/clear sailing

MEANING: when something is easy and moving forward without complications

EXAMPLE: Once I finish my presentation, the Q&A session will be smooth sailing.

EXPRESSION:

MEANING:

EXAMPLES:

EXPRESSION: snail mail

MEANING: traditional post office mail, such as letters and packages

EXAMPLE: You have to send accounting the original receipts by snail mail. They don't accept scanned receipts.

EXPRESSION:

MEANING:

EXAMPLES:

EXPRESSION: stand one's ground

MEANING: to not change your opinion or stance

EXAMPLE: We tried to change the work from home policy but HR stood their ground and denied the request.

EXPRESSION:

MEANING:

EXAMPLES:

EXPRESSION: start/got off on the right foot

MEANING: to start something in a good and positive way

EXAMPLE: Spilling coffee on my new boss was not starting off on the right foot.

EXPRESSION:

MEANING:

EXAMPLES:

EXPRESSION: start/got off on the wrong foot

MEANING: to start something poorly or in a negative way

EXAMPLE: John really got off on the wrong foot when he insulted his new coworker.

EXPRESSION:

MEANING:

EXAMPLES:

EXPRESSION: state of the art

MEANING: most advanced

EXAMPLE: CERN in Switzerland is a state-of-the-art particle accelerator facility.

<hr>

EXPRESSION:

MEANING:

EXAMPLES:

EXPRESSION: take something lying down

MEANING: to accept something unpleasant without putting up a fight

EXAMPLE: We can't take it lying down. We're going to fight Facebook's new policy or we're going to cancel all our advertising with them.

EXPRESSION:

MEANING:

EXAMPLES:

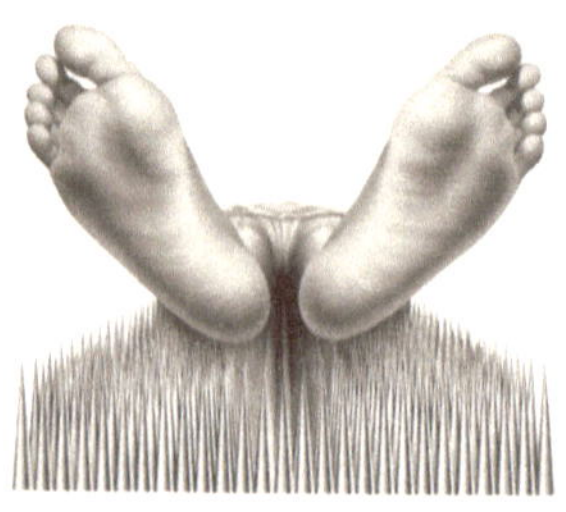

EXPRESSION: take the bull by the horns

MEANING: to take control of a situation

EXAMPLE: Sometimes you just have to take the bull by the horns and make it happen.

EXPRESSION:

MEANING:

EXAMPLES:

EXPRESSION: talk someone into something

MEANING: to convince someone to do something

EXAMPLE: We talked the boss into giving us the day off after we won the company sales contest.

EXPRESSION:

MEANING:

EXAMPLES:

EXPRESSION: talk someone out of something

MEANING: to convince someone not to do something

EXAMPLE: I wanted to invest in the futures market but my banker talked me out of it.

EXPRESSION:

MEANING:

EXAMPLES:

EXPRESSION: the elephant in the room

MEANING: a big or obvious problem or situation that nobody wants to address

EXAMPLE: I know no one wants to talk about the elephant in the room, but we must deal with our financial situation before it deals with us.

EXPRESSION:

MEANING:

EXAMPLES:

EXPRESSION: think big

MEANING: to have big ideas, plans, ambitions, or goals

EXAMPLE: If we don't think big, we'll never succeed in this business.

EXPRESSION:

MEANING:

EXAMPLES:

EXPRESSION: think outside the box

MEANING: to think creatively from a new perspective

EXAMPLE: She was really thinking outside the box when she came up with that unique marketing campaign.

EXPRESSION:

MEANING:

EXAMPLES:

EXPRESSION: throw in the towel

MEANING: to quit or give up

EXAMPLE: I was trying to learn English, but I got frustrated and threw in the towel.

EXPRESSION:

MEANING:

EXAMPLES:

EXPRESSION: time's up

MEANING: an event or appointment has come to an end

EXAMPLE: After the no confidence vote, his time's up as prime minister and parliament will soon replace him.

EXPRESSION:

MEANING:

EXAMPLES:

EXPRESSION: touch base

MEANING: to check in with or make contact with someone

EXAMPLE: Let's touch base tomorrow to discuss how things are progressing.

EXPRESSION:

MEANING:

EXAMPLES:

EXPRESSION: twist someone's arm

MEANING: to convince or coerce someone into doing something they don't want to do

EXAMPLE: We had to twist his arm to cough up his share of the dinner bill.

EXPRESSION:

MEANING:

EXAMPLES:

EXPRESSION: under the table

MEANING: a business activity done secretly, often illegally

EXAMPLE: Our competitor frequently pays his employees under the table to avoid paying employment taxes.

EXPRESSION:

MEANING:

EXAMPLES:

EXPRESSION: up in the air

MEANING: when something is undecided or the potential outcome is unknown

EXAMPLE: Everything is up in the air until the next board meeting.

EXPRESSION:

MEANING:

EXAMPLES:

EXPRESSION: uphill battle

MEANING: difficult to accomplish

EXAMPLE: It's an uphill battle to get the accounting department to approve my expenses.

EXPRESSION:

MEANING:

EXAMPLES:

EXPRESSION: upper hand

MEANING: an advantage

EXAMPLE: George always has the upper hand playing poker because he used to work in a casino.

EXPRESSION:

MEANING:

EXAMPLES:

EXPRESSION: win-win situation

MEANING: everyone involved benefits, or every potential outcome is positive

EXAMPLE: Cutting costs while improving the product is a win-win situation for us and our customers.

EXPRESSION:

MEANING:

EXAMPLES:

EXPRESSION: word of mouth

MEANING: information travelling through informal conversation with family, friends, etc.

EXAMPLE: Word of mouth advertising is worth more to our company than spending big bucks on a TV campaign.

EXPRESSION:

MEANING:

EXAMPLES:

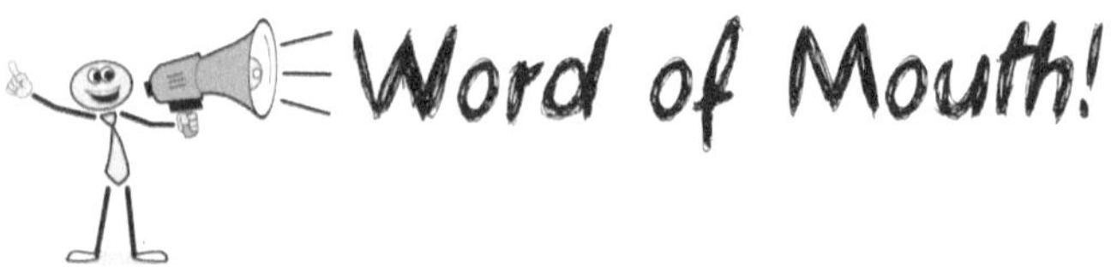

EXPRESSION: writing on the wall

MEANING: evidence and indications that something (often negative) is going to happen

EXAMPLE: You can't ignore the writing on the wall. If sales continue to fall, the business is going to fail.

EXPRESSION:

MEANING:

EXAMPLES:

EXPRESSION: yes man

MEANING: someone who always agrees with you

EXAMPLE: My boss is so insecure he always surrounds himself with yes men.

EXPRESSION:

MEANING:

EXAMPLES:

www.ingramcontent.com/pod-product-compliance
Lightning Source LLC
Chambersburg PA
CBHW062225150726
47991CB00006B/2447